Instructions for Use

Welcome! This journal was designed to be used with the Magic Spells: Intentional Spells for Modern Witches. However, it's a great resource for meditation and mindfulness.

Use the index to keep your entries organized and track things like your mood, conflicts, dreams, and other signs. There's a lined page before each set of journal prompts that you can use to write the spell used and any other pertinent notes.

Enjoy!

my index ———————————————————

Topic/Spell	Page(s)

my index

Topic/Spell	Page(s)

my index

Topic/Spell	Page(s)

my index

Topic/Spell	Page(s)

SPELL: _____   **DATE:** _____

INGREDIENTS AND PREPARATION

Ideal Setting
_____

Ingredients
_____

Preparation/Instructions
_____

JOURNALING PROMPTS

A. What is your target? Why have you chosen this?

_____

_____

_____

_____

B. What sacrifice are you prepared to make?

_____

_____

_____

_____

C. Why do you feel that you need guidance, inspiration, and/or strength?

_____

_____

_____

_____

D. Name 3 things that are you willing to sacrifice or do in exchange for help? Rank them from most difficult to least.

_____

_____

_____

_____

E. What beliefs and skills are you already bringing to the universe in this area?

_____

_____

_____

_____

F. Once a scale of 1 - 10, how likely do you believe you'd succeed in this area without intervention? What's the basis for your estimate?

_____

_____

_____

_____

G. What serious roadblock do you need to confront in order to move forward? What's kept you from addressing this sooner?

_____

_____

_____

_____

H. About how long do you think it would take the universe to rearrange things to your favor? For instance, things like significant weight loss or a legal case could take many months to resolve.

I. _____

responded to your request.

J. In what way could your desire not align with the Universe's? For example, does someone else have an equally pressing reason for a different outcome? Is your claim superior? Why or why not?

K. How long are you willing to wait for an answer?

L. How will you cope if your spell is ineffective?

M. How you promise to thank the universe and benefit others if your spell succeeds?

PRE-SPELL PERFORMANCE

N. Describe your mood.

_____

_____

O. How relaxed are you on a scale from 1 (least relaxed) - 10? _____

P. Do you sense any potential blockages or have any concerns about your ability to successfully cast this spell??

_____

_____

_____

Q. Where will you cast this spell?

_____

R. Will anyone else be in the vicinity?

_____

S. How will you set the mood?

_____

_____

T. Are there any changes/substitutions will you be making? If so, what?

_____

_____

POST-SPELL REVIEW

U. Where you able to maintain focus and perform the spell flawlessly? If not, what happened?

_____

_____

_____

_____

V. What emotions did you feel during your preparation and performance?

_____

_____

_____

_____

W. Dreams/Other Potential Signs from the Universe I Write or Sketch below.

_____

_____

_____

_____

_____

_____

_____

_____

RESULTS

X. How would you rate your experience on a scale from 1 (negative experience) - 10 (positive experience)? _____

Y. Was the spell successful? Why or why not?

_____

_____

_____

_____

Z. If you had to cast the spell again, are there any elements (e.g. ingredients, invocation, etc.) that you'd like to adapt/change?

_____

_____

_____

_____

SPELL: _____ **DATE:** _____

INGREDIENTS AND PREPARATION

Ideal Setting
_____

Ingredients
_____

Preparation/Instructions
_____

A. _____

B. What sacrifice are you prepared to make?

C. Why do you feel that you need guidance, inspiration, and/or strength?

D. Name 3 things that are you willing to sacrifice or do in exchange for help? Rank them from most difficult to least.

E. What beliefs and skills are you already bringing to the universe in this area?

_____

_____

_____

_____

F. Once a scale of 1 - 10, how likely do you believe you'd succeed in this area without intervention? What's the basis for your estimate?

_____

_____

_____

_____

G. What serious roadblock do you need to confront in order to move forward? What's kept you from addressing this sooner?

_____

_____

_____

_____

H. About how long do you think it would take the universe to rearrange things to your favor? For instance, things like significant weight loss or a legal case could take many months to resolve.

I. _____

responded to your request.

J. In what way could your desire not align with the Universe's? For example, does someone else have an equally pressing reason for a different outcome? Is your claim superior? Why or why not?

K. How long are you willing to wait for an answer?

L. How will you cope if your spell is ineffective?

M. How you promise to thank the universe and benefit others if your spell succeeds?

PRE-SPELL PERFORMANCE

N. Describe your mood.

_____

_____

O. How relaxed are you on a scale from 1 (least relaxed) - 10? _____

P. Do you sense any potential blockages or have any concerns about your ability to successfully cast this spell??

_____

_____

_____

Q. Where will you cast this spell?

_____

R. Will anyone else be in the vicinity?

_____

S. How will you set the mood?

_____

_____

T. Are there any changes/substitutions will you be making? If so, what?

_____

_____

POST-SPELL REVIEW

U. Where you able to maintain focus and perform the spell flawlessly? If not, what happened?

_____

_____

_____

_____

V. What emotions did you feel during your preparation and performance?

_____

_____

_____

_____

_____

W. Dreams/Other Potential Signs from the Universe | Write or Sketch below.

_____

_____

_____

_____

_____

_____

_____

_____

_____

_____

RESULTS

X. How would you rate your experience on a scale from 1 (negative experience) - 10 (positive experience)? _____

Y. Was the spell successful? Why or why not?

_____

_____

_____

_____

Z. If you had to cast the spell again, are there any elements (e.g. ingredients, invocation, etc.) that you'd like to adapt/change?

_____

_____

_____

SPELL: _____ **DATE:** _____

INGREDIENTS AND PREPARATION

Ideal Setting

_____

Ingredients

_____

A.

B. What sacrifice are you prepared to make?

C. Why do you feel that you need guidance, inspiration, and/or strength?

D. Name 3 things that are you willing to sacrifice or do in exchange for help? Rank them from most difficult to least.

E. What beliefs and skills are you already bringing to the universe in this area?

F. Once a scale of 1 - 10, how likely do you believe you'd succeed in this area without intervention? What's the basis for your estimate?

G. What serious roadblock do you need to confront in order to move forward? What's kept you from addressing this sooner?

H. About how long do you think it would take the universe to rearrange things to your favor? For instance, things like significant weight loss or a legal case could take many months to resolve.

I. --

responded to your request.

J. In what way could your desire not align with the Universe's? For example, does someone else have an equally pressing reason for a different outcome? Is your claim superior? Why or why not?

K. How long are you willing to wait for an answer?

L. How will you cope if your spell is ineffective?

M. How you promise to thank the universe and benefit others if your spell succeeds?

\

PRE-SPELL PERFORMANCE

N. Describe your mood.

_____

_____

O. How relaxed are you on a scale from 1 (least relaxed) - 10? _____

P. Do you sense any potential blockages or have any concerns about your ability to successfully cast this spell??

_____

_____

_____

Q. Where will you cast this spell?

_____

R. Will anyone else be in the vicinity?

_____

S. How will you set the mood?

_____

_____

T. Are there any changes/substitutions will you be making? If so, what?

_____

_____

POST-SPELL REVIEW

U. Where you able to maintain focus and perform the spell flawlessly? If not, what happened?

_____

_____

_____

_____

V. What emotions did you feel during your preparation and performance?

_____

_____

_____

_____

_____

W. Dreams/Other Potential Signs from the Universe I Write or Sketch below.

_____

_____

_____

_____

_____

_____

_____

_____

RESULTS

X. How would you rate your experience on a scale from 1 (negative experience) - 10 (positive experience)? _____

Y. Was the spell successful? Why or why not?

_____

_____

_____

_____

Z. If you had to cast the spell again, are there any elements (e.g. ingredients, invocation, etc.) that you'd like to adapt/change?

_____

_____

_____

_____

SPELL: _____ **DATE:** _____

INGREDIENTS AND PREPARATION

Ideal Setting
_____

Ingredients
_____

Preparation/Instructions
_____

A.

_____

_____

_____

_____

B. What sacrifice are you prepared to make?

_____

_____

_____

_____

C. Why do you feel that you need guidance, inspiration, and/or strength?

_____

_____

_____

_____

D. Name 3 things that are you willing to sacrifice or do in exchange for help? Rank them from most difficult to least.

_____

_____

_____

_____

E. What beliefs and skills are you already bringing to the universe in this area?

F. Once a scale of 1 - 10, how likely do you believe you'd succeed in this area without intervention? What's the basis for your estimate?

G. What serious roadblock do you need to confront in order to move forward? What's kept you from addressing this sooner?

H. About how long do you think it would take the universe to rearrange things to your favor? For instance, things like significant weight loss or a legal case could take many months to resolve.

I.

responded to your request.

J. In what way could your desire not align with the Universe's? For example, does someone else have an equally pressing reason for a different outcome? Is your claim superior? Why or why not?

K. How long are you willing to wait for an answer?

L. How will you cope if your spell is ineffective?

M. How you promise to thank the universe and benefit others if your spell succeeds?

PRE-SPELL PERFORMANCE

N. Describe your mood.

_____

_____

O. How relaxed are you on a scale from 1 (least relaxed) - 10? _____

P. Do you sense any potential blockages or have any concerns about your ability to successfully cast this spell??

_____

_____

_____

Q. Where will you cast this spell?

_____

_____

R. Will anyone else be in the vicinity?

_____

S. How will you set the mood?

_____

_____

T. Are there any changes/substitutions will you be making? If so, what?

_____

_____

POST-SPELL REVIEW

U. Where you able to maintain focus and perform the spell flawlessly? If not, what happened?

V. What emotions did you feel during your preparation and performance?

W. Dreams/Other Potential Signs from the Universe I Write or Sketch below.

RESULTS

X. How would you rate your experience on a scale from 1 (negative experience) - 10 (positive experience)? _____

Y. Was the spell successful? Why or why not?

_____

_____

_____

_____

Z. If you had to cast the spell again, are there any elements (e.g. ingredients, invocation, etc.) that you'd like to adapt/change?

_____

_____

_____

_____

SPELL: _____ **DATE:** _____

INGREDIENTS AND PREPARATION

Ideal Setting
_____

Ingredients
_____

Preparation/Instructions
_____

A.

B. What sacrifice are you prepared to make?

C. Why do you feel that you need guidance, inspiration, and/or strength?

D. Name 3 things that are you willing to sacrifice or do in exchange for help? Rank them from most difficult to least.

E. What beliefs and skills are you already bringing to the universe in this area?

_____

_____

_____

_____

F. Once a scale of 1 - 10, how likely do you believe you'd succeed in this area without intervention? What's the basis for your estimate?

_____

_____

_____

_____

G. What serious roadblock do you need to confront in order to move forward? What's kept you from addressing this sooner?

_____

_____

_____

_____

H. About how long do you think it would take the universe to rearrange things to your favor? For instance, things like significant weight loss or a legal case could take many months to resolve.

I. _____

responded to your request.

J. In what way could your desire not align with the Universe's? For example, does someone else have an equally pressing reason for a different outcome? Is your claim superior? Why or why not?

K. How long are you willing to wait for an answer?

L. How will you cope if your spell is ineffective?

M. How you promise to thank the universe and benefit others if your spell succeeds?

PRE-SPELL PERFORMANCE

N. Describe your mood.

_____

_____

O. How relaxed are you on a scale from 1 (least relaxed) - 10? _____

P. Do you sense any potential blockages or have any concerns about your ability to successfully cast this spell??

_____

_____

_____

Q. Where will you cast this spell?

_____

R. Will anyone else be in the vicinity?

_____

S. How will you set the mood?

_____

_____

T. Are there any changes/substitutions will you be making? If so, what?

_____

_____

POST-SPELL REVIEW

U. Where you able to maintain focus and perform the spell flawlessly? If not, what happened?

_____

_____

_____

_____

V. What emotions did you feel during your preparation and performance?

_____

_____

_____

_____

W. Dreams/Other Potential Signs from the Universe | Write or Sketch below.

_____

_____

_____

_____

_____

_____

_____

_____

RESULTS

X. How would you rate your experience on a scale from 1 (negative experience) - 10 (positive experience)? _____

Y. Was the spell successful? Why or why not?

_____

_____

_____

_____

Z. If you had to cast the spell again, are there any elements (e.g. ingredients, invocation, etc.) that you'd like to adapt/change?

_____

_____

_____

_____

SPELL: _____ **DATE:** _____

INGREDIENTS AND PREPARATION

Ideal Setting
_____

Ingredients
_____

Preparation/Instructions
_____

A.

_____

_____

_____

_____

_____

B. What sacrifice are you prepared to make?

_____

_____

_____

_____

C. Why do you feel that you need guidance, inspiration, and/or strength?

_____

_____

_____

_____

D. Name 3 things that are you willing to sacrifice or do in exchange for help? Rank them from most difficult to least.

_____

_____

_____

_____

E. What beliefs and skills are you already bringing to the universe in this area?

F. Once a scale of 1 - 10, how likely do you believe you'd succeed in this area without intervention? What's the basis for your estimate?

G. What serious roadblock do you need to confront in order to move forward? What's kept you from addressing this sooner?

H. About how long do you think it would take the universe to rearrange things to your favor? For instance, things like significant weight loss or a legal case could take many months to resolve.

I.

responded to your request.

J. In what way could your desire not align with the Universe's? For example, does someone else have an equally pressing reason for a different outcome? Is your claim superior? Why or why not?

K. How long are you willing to wait for an answer?

L. How will you cope if your spell is ineffective?

M. How you promise to thank the universe and benefit others if your spell succeeds?

PRE-SPELL PERFORMANCE

N. Describe your mood.

_____

_____

O. How relaxed are you on a scale from 1 (least relaxed) - 10? _____

P. Do you sense any potential blockages or have any concerns about your ability to successfully cast this spell??

_____

_____

_____

Q. Where will you cast this spell?

_____

R. Will anyone else be in the vicinity?

_____

S. How will you set the mood?

_____

_____

T. Are there any changes/substitutions will you be making? If so, what?

_____

_____

_____

POST-SPELL REVIEW

U. Where you able to maintain focus and perform the spell flawlessly? If not, what happened?

_____

_____

_____

_____

V. What emotions did you feel during your preparation and performance?

_____

_____

_____

_____

W. Dreams/Other Potential Signs from the Universe I Write or Sketch below.

_____

_____

_____

_____

_____

_____

_____

_____

RESULTS

X. How would you rate your experience on a scale from 1 (negative experience) - 10 (positive experience)? _____

Y. Was the spell successful? Why or why not?

_____

_____

_____

_____

Z. If you had to cast the spell again, are there any elements (e.g. ingredients, invocation, etc.) that you'd like to adapt/change?

_____

_____

_____

_____

SPELL: _____ **DATE:** _____

INGREDIENTS AND PREPARATION

Ideal Setting

_____

Ingredients

_____

Preparation/Instructions

_____

A.

B. What sacrifice are you prepared to make?

C. Why do you feel that you need guidance, inspiration, and/or strength?

D. Name 3 things that are you willing to sacrifice or do in exchange for help? Rank them from most difficult to least.

E. What beliefs and skills are you already bringing to the universe in this area?

_____

_____

_____

_____

_____

F. Once a scale of 1 - 10, how likely do you believe you'd succeed in this area without intervention? What's the basis for your estimate?

_____

_____

_____

_____

_____

G. What serious roadblock do you need to confront in order to move forward? What's kept you from addressing this sooner?

_____

_____

_____

_____

H. About how long do you think it would take the universe to rearrange things to your favor? For instance, things like significant weight loss or a legal case could take many months to resolve.

I. _____

responded to your request.

J. In what way could your desire not align with the Universe's? For example, does someone else have an equally pressing reason for a different outcome? Is your claim superior? Why or why not?

K. How long are you willing to wait for an answer?

L. How will you cope if your spell is ineffective?

M. How you promise to thank the universe and benefit others if your spell succeeds?

PRE-SPELL PERFORMANCE

N. Describe your mood.

_____

_____

O. How relaxed are you on a scale from 1 (least relaxed) - 10? _____

P. Do you sense any potential blockages or have any concerns about your ability to successfully cast this spell??

_____

_____

_____

Q. Where will you cast this spell?

_____

R. Will anyone else be in the vicinity?

_____

S. How will you set the mood?

_____

_____

T. Are there any changes/substitutions will you be making? If so, what?

_____

_____

POST-SPELL REVIEW

U. Where you able to maintain focus and perform the spell flawlessly? If not, what happened?

_____

_____

_____

_____

V. What emotions did you feel during your preparation and performance?

_____

_____

_____

_____

_____

W. Dreams/Other Potential Signs from the Universe I Write or Sketch below.

_____

_____

_____

_____

_____

_____

_____

_____

_____

_____

RESULTS

X. How would you rate your experience on a scale from 1 (negative experience) - 10 (positive experience)? _____

Y. Was the spell successful? Why or why not?

_____

_____

_____

_____

Z. If you had to cast the spell again, are there any elements (e.g. ingredients, invocation, etc.) that you'd like to adapt/change?

_____

_____

_____

_____

SPELL: _____ **DATE:** _____

INGREDIENTS AND PREPARATION

Ideal Setting
_____

Ingredients
_____

Preparation/Instructions
_____

A.

B. What sacrifice are you prepared to make?

C. Why do you feel that you need guidance, inspiration, and/or strength?

D. Name 3 things that are you willing to sacrifice or do in exchange for help? Rank them from most difficult to least.

E. What beliefs and skills are you already bringing to the universe in this area?

_____

_____

_____

_____

F. Once a scale of 1 - 10, how likely do you believe you'd succeed in this area without intervention? What's the basis for your estimate?

_____

_____

_____

_____

G. What serious roadblock do you need to confront in order to move forward? What's kept you from addressing this sooner?

_____

_____

_____

_____

H. About how long do you think it would take the universe to rearrange things to your favor? For instance, things like significant weight loss or a legal case could take many months to resolve.

I. _____

responded to your request.

J. In what way could your desire not align with the Universe's? For example, does someone else have an equally pressing reason for a different outcome? Is your claim superior? Why or why not?

K. How long are you willing to wait for an answer?

L. How will you cope if your spell is ineffective?

M. How you promise to thank the universe and benefit others if your spell succeeds?

PRE-SPELL PERFORMANCE

N. Describe your mood.

_____

_____

O. How relaxed are you on a scale from 1 (least relaxed) - 10? _____

P. Do you sense any potential blockages or have any concerns about your ability to successfully cast this spell??

_____

_____

_____

Q. Where will you cast this spell?

_____

R. Will anyone else be in the vicinity?

_____

S. How will you set the mood?

_____

_____

T. Are there any changes/substitutions will you be making? If so, what?

_____

_____

POST-SPELL REVIEW

U. Where you able to maintain focus and perform the spell flawlessly? If not, what happened?

_____

_____

_____

_____

V. What emotions did you feel during your preparation and performance?

_____

_____

_____

_____

W. Dreams/Other Potential Signs from the Universe I Write or Sketch below.

_____

_____

_____

_____

_____

_____

_____

_____

RESULTS

X. How would you rate your experience on a scale from 1 (negative experience) - 10 (positive experience)? _____

Y. Was the spell successful? Why or why not?

_____

_____

_____

_____

Z. If you had to cast the spell again, are there any elements (e.g. ingredients, invocation, etc.) that you'd like to adapt/change?

_____

_____

_____

_____

SPELL: _____   **DATE:** _____

INGREDIENTS AND PREPARATION

Ideal Setting
_____

Ingredients
_____

Preparation/Instructions
_____

JOURNALING PROMPTS

A. What is your target? Why have you chosen this?

B. What sacrifice are you prepared to make?

C. Why do you feel that you need guidance, inspiration, and/or strength?

D. Name 3 things that are you willing to sacrifice or do in exchange for help? Rank them from most difficult to least.

E. What beliefs and skills are you already bringing to the universe in this area?

F. Once a scale of 1 - 10, how likely do you believe you'd succeed in this area without intervention? What's the basis for your estimate?

G. What serious roadblock do you need to confront in order to move forward? What's kept you from addressing this sooner?

H. About how long do you think it would take the universe to rearrange things to your favor? For instance, things like significant weight loss or a legal case could take many months to resolve.

I.

responded to your request.

J. In what way could your desire not align with the Universe's? For example, does someone else have an equally pressing reason for a different outcome? Is your claim superior? Why or why not?

K. How long are you willing to wait for an answer?

L. How will you cope if your spell is ineffective?

M. How you promise to thank the universe and benefit others if your spell succeeds?

PRE-SPELL PERFORMANCE

N. Describe your mood.

_____

_____

O. How relaxed are you on a scale from 1 (least relaxed) - 10? _____

P. Do you sense any potential blockages or have any concerns about your ability to successfully cast this spell??

_____

_____

_____

Q. Where will you cast this spell?

_____

R. Will anyone else be in the vicinity?

_____

S. How will you set the mood?

_____

_____

T. Are there any changes/substitutions will you be making? If so, what?

_____

_____

_____

POST-SPELL REVIEW

U. Where you able to maintain focus and perform the spell flawlessly? If not, what happened?

_____

_____

_____

_____

V. What emotions did you feel during your preparation and performance?

_____

_____

_____

_____

W. Dreams/Other Potential Signs from the Universe | Write or Sketch below.

_____

_____

_____

_____

_____

_____

_____

_____

RESULTS

X. How would you rate your experience on a scale from 1 (negative experience) - 10 (positive experience)? _____

Y. Was the spell successful? Why or why not?

_____

_____

_____

_____

Z. If you had to cast the spell again, are there any elements (e.g. ingredients, invocation, etc.) that you'd like to adapt/change?

_____

_____

_____

_____

SPELL: _____   **DATE:** _____

INGREDIENTS AND PREPARATION

Ideal Setting
_____

Ingredients
_____

Preparation/Instructions
_____

A.

_____

B. What sacrifice are you prepared to make?

_____

C. Why do you feel that you need guidance, inspiration, and/or strength?

_____

D. Name 3 things that are you willing to sacrifice or do in exchange for help? Rank them from most difficult to least.

_____

E. What beliefs and skills are you already bringing to the universe in this area?

F. Once a scale of 1 - 10, how likely do you believe you'd succeed in this area without intervention? What's the basis for your estimate?

G. What serious roadblock do you need to confront in order to move forward? What's kept you from addressing this sooner?

H. About how long do you think it would take the universe to rearrange things to your favor? For instance, things like significant weight loss or a legal case could take many months to resolve.

I.

responded to your request.

_____

_____

_____

_____

_____

_____

_____

J. In what way could your desire not align with the Universe's? For example, does someone else have an equally pressing reason for a different outcome? Is your claim superior? Why or why not?

_____

_____

_____

_____

K. How long are you willing to wait for an answer?

_____

L. How will you cope if your spell is ineffective?

_____

_____

_____

_____

M. How you promise to thank the universe and benefit others if your spell succeeds?

PRE-SPELL PERFORMANCE

N. Describe your mood.

_____

_____

O. How relaxed are you on a scale from 1 (least relaxed) - 10? _____

P. Do you sense any potential blockages or have any concerns about your ability to successfully cast this spell??

_____

_____

_____

Q. Where will you cast this spell?

_____

R. Will anyone else be in the vicinity?

_____

S. How will you set the mood?

_____

_____

T. Are there any changes/substitutions will you be making? If so, what?

_____

_____

POST-SPELL REVIEW

U. Where you able to maintain focus and perform the spell flawlessly? If not, what happened?

_____

_____

_____

_____

V. What emotions did you feel during your preparation and performance?

_____

_____

_____

_____

W. Dreams/Other Potential Signs from the Universe | Write or Sketch below.

_____

_____

_____

_____

_____

_____

_____

_____

RESULTS

X. How would you rate your experience on a scale from 1 (negative experience) - 10 (positive experience)? _____

Y. Was the spell successful? Why or why not?

_____
_____
_____
_____

Z. If you had to cast the spell again, are there any elements (e.g. ingredients, invocation, etc.) that you'd like to adapt/change?

_____
_____
_____
_____

SPELL: _____ **DATE:** _____

INGREDIENTS AND PREPARATION

Ideal Setting
_____

Ingredients
_____

Preparation/Instructions
_____

JOURNALING PROMPTS

A. What is your target? Why have you chosen this?

_____

_____

_____

_____

B. What sacrifice are you prepared to make?

_____

_____

_____

_____

C. Why do you feel that you need guidance, inspiration, and/or strength?

_____

_____

_____

_____

D. Name 3 things that are you willing to sacrifice or do in exchange for help? Rank them from most difficult to least.

_____

_____

_____

_____

E. What beliefs and skills are you already bringing to the universe in this area?

_____

_____

_____

_____

F. Once a scale of 1 - 10, how likely do you believe you'd succeed in this area without intervention? What's the basis for your estimate?

_____

_____

_____

_____

G. What serious roadblock do you need to confront in order to move forward? What's kept you from addressing this sooner?

_____

_____

_____

_____

H. About how long do you think it would take the universe to rearrange things to your favor? For instance, things like significant weight loss or a legal case could take many months to resolve.

I. _____

responded to your request.

_____

_____

_____

_____

_____

_____

_____

J. In what way could your desire not align with the Universe's? For example, does someone else have an equally pressing reason for a different outcome? Is your claim superior? Why or why not?

_____

_____

_____

_____

_____

K. How long are you willing to wait for an answer?

_____

L. How will you cope if your spell is ineffective?

_____

_____

_____

_____

M. How you promise to thank the universe and benefit others if your spell succeeds?

PRE-SPELL PERFORMANCE

N. Describe your mood.

_____

_____

O. How relaxed are you on a scale from 1 (least relaxed) - 10? _____

P. Do you sense any potential blockages or have any concerns about your ability to successfully cast this spell??

_____

_____

_____

Q. Where will you cast this spell?

_____

R. Will anyone else be in the vicinity?

_____

S. How will you set the mood?

_____

_____

T. Are there any changes/substitutions will you be making? If so, what?

_____

_____

_____

POST-SPELL REVIEW

U. Where you able to maintain focus and perform the spell flawlessly? If not, what happened?

_____

_____

_____

_____

V. What emotions did you feel during your preparation and performance?

_____

_____

_____

_____

W. Dreams/Other Potential Signs from the Universe I Write or Sketch below.

_____

_____

_____

_____

_____

_____

_____

RESULTS

X. How would you rate your experience on a scale from 1 (negative experience) - 10 (positive experience)? _____

Y. Was the spell successful? Why or why not?

_____

_____

_____

_____

Z. If you had to cast the spell again, are there any elements (e.g. ingredients, invocation, etc.) that you'd like to adapt/change?

_____

_____

_____

_____

SPELL: _____   **DATE:** _____

INGREDIENTS AND PREPARATION

Ideal Setting
_____

Ingredients
_____

Preparation/Instructions
_____

A.

B. What sacrifice are you prepared to make?

C. Why do you feel that you need guidance, inspiration, and/or strength?

D. Name 3 things that are you willing to sacrifice or do in exchange for help? Rank them from most difficult to least.

E. What beliefs and skills are you already bringing to the universe in this area?

_____

_____

_____

_____

F. Once a scale of 1 - 10, how likely do you believe you'd succeed in this area without intervention? What's the basis for your estimate?

_____

_____

_____

_____

G. What serious roadblock do you need to confront in order to move forward? What's kept you from addressing this sooner?

_____

_____

_____

_____

H. About how long do you think it would take the universe to rearrange things to your favor? For instance, things like significant weight loss or a legal case could take many months to resolve.

I. _____

responded to your request.

J. In what way could your desire not align with the Universe's? For example, does someone else have an equally pressing reason for a different outcome? Is your claim superior? Why or why not?

K. How long are you willing to wait for an answer?

L. How will you cope if your spell is ineffective?

M. How you promise to thank the universe and benefit others if your spell succeeds?

PRE-SPELL PERFORMANCE

N. Describe your mood.

_____

_____

O. How relaxed are you on a scale from 1 (least relaxed) - 10? _____

P. Do you sense any potential blockages or have any concerns about your ability to successfully cast this spell??

_____

_____

_____

Q. Where will you cast this spell?

_____

R. Will anyone else be in the vicinity?

_____

S. How will you set the mood?

_____

_____

T. Are there any changes/substitutions will you be making? If so, what?

_____

_____

_____

POST-SPELL REVIEW

U. Where you able to maintain focus and perform the spell flawlessly? If not, what happened?

_____

_____

_____

_____

V. What emotions did you feel during your preparation and performance?

_____

_____

_____

W. Dreams/Other Potential Signs from the Universe | Write or Sketch below.

_____

_____

_____

_____

_____

_____

_____

RESULTS

X. How would you rate your experience on a scale from 1 (negative experience) - 10 (positive experience)? _____

Y. Was the spell successful? Why or why not?

_____

_____

_____

_____

Z. If you had to cast the spell again, are there any elements (e.g. ingredients, invocation, etc.) that you'd like to adapt/change?

_____

_____

_____

_____

SPELL: _____ **DATE:** _____

INGREDIENTS AND PREPARATION

Ideal Setting
_____

Ingredients
_____

Preparation/Instructions
_____

A.

B. What sacrifice are you prepared to make?

C. Why do you feel that you need guidance, inspiration, and/or strength?

D. Name 3 things that are you willing to sacrifice or do in exchange for help? Rank them from most difficult to least.

E. What beliefs and skills are you already bringing to the universe in this area?

_____

_____

_____

_____

F. Once a scale of 1 - 10, how likely do you believe you'd succeed in this area without intervention? What's the basis for your estimate?

_____

_____

_____

_____orward?

_____

_____

_____

_____

_____

H. About how long do you think it would take the universe to rearrange things to your favor? For instance, things like significant weight loss or a legal case could take many months to resolve.

I. _____

responded to your request.

J. In what way could your desire not align with the Universe's? For example, does someone else have an equally pressing reason for a different outcome? Is your claim superior? Why or why not?

K. How long are you willing to wait for an answer?

L. How will you cope if your spell is ineffective?

M. How you promise to thank the universe and benefit others if your spell succeeds?

PRE-SPELL PERFORMANCE

N. Describe your mood.

_____

_____

O. How relaxed are you on a scale from 1 (least relaxed) - 10? _____

P. Do you sense any potential blockages or have any concerns about your ability to successfully cast this spell??

_____

_____

_____

Q. Where will you cast this spell?

_____

R. Will anyone else be in the vicinity?

_____

S. How will you set the mood?

_____

_____

T. Are there any changes/substitutions will you be making? If so, what?

_____

_____

POST-SPELL REVIEW

U. Where you able to maintain focus and perform the spell flawlessly? If not, what happened?

V. What emotions did you feel during your preparation and performance?

W. Dreams/Other Potential Signs from the Universe I Write or Sketch below.

RESULTS

X. How would you rate your experience on a scale from 1 (negative experience) -
10 (positive experience)? _____

Y. Was the spell successful? Why or why not?

_____

_____

_____

_____

Z. If you had to cast the spell again, are there any elements (e.g. ingredients,
invocation, etc.) that you'd like to adapt/change?

_____

_____

_____

_____

SPELL: _____   **DATE:** _____

INGREDIENTS AND PREPARATION

Ideal Setting
_____

Ingredients
_____

Preparation/Instructions
_____

JOURNALING PROMPTS

A. What is your target? Why have you chosen this?

B. What sacrifice are you prepared to make?

C. Why do you feel that you need guidance, inspiration, and/or strength?

D. Name 3 things that are you willing to sacrifice or do in exchange for help? Rank them from most difficult to least.

E. What beliefs and skills are you already bringing to the universe in this area?

_____

_____

_____

_____

F. Once a scale of 1 - 10, how likely do you believe you'd succeed in this area without intervention? What's the basis for your estimate?

_____

_____

_____

_____

G. What serious roadblock do you need to confront in order to move forward? What's kept you from addressing this sooner?

_____

_____

_____

_____

H. About how long do you think it would take the universe to rearrange things to your favor? For instance, things like significant weight loss or a legal case could take many months to resolve.

I. _____

responded to your request.

J. In what way could your desire not align with the Universe's? For example, does someone else have an equally pressing reason for a different outcome? Is your claim superior? Why or why not?

K. How long are you willing to wait for an answer?

L. How will you cope if your spell is ineffective?

M. How you promise to thank the universe and benefit others if your spell succeeds?

PRE-SPELL PERFORMANCE

N. Describe your mood.

_____

_____

O. How relaxed are you on a scale from 1 (least relaxed) - 10? _____

P. Do you sense any potential blockages or have any concerns about your ability to successfully cast this spell??

_____

_____

_____

Q. Where will you cast this spell?

_____

R. Will anyone else be in the vicinity?

_____

S. How will you set the mood?

_____

_____

T. Are there any changes/substitutions will you be making? If so, what?

_____

_____

_____

POST-SPELL REVIEW

U. Where you able to maintain focus and perform the spell flawlessly? If not, what happened?

_____

_____

_____

_____

V. What emotions did you feel during your preparation and performance?

_____

_____

_____

_____

W. Dreams/Other Potential Signs from the Universe I Write or Sketch below.

_____

_____

_____

_____

_____

_____

_____

_____

RESULTS

X. How would you rate your experience on a scale from 1 (negative experience) - 10 (positive experience)? _____

Y. Was the spell successful? Why or why not?

_____

_____

_____

_____

Z. If you had to cast the spell again, are there any elements (e.g. ingredients, invocation, etc.) that you'd like to adapt/change?

_____

_____

_____

_____

SPELL: _____   **DATE:** _____

INGREDIENTS AND PREPARATION

Ideal Setting
_____

Ingredients
_____

Preparation/Instructions
_____

JOURNALING PROMPTS

A. What is your target? Why have you chosen this?

_____

_____

_____

_____

_____

B. What sacrifice are you prepared to make?

_____

_____

_____

_____

_____

C. Why do you feel that you need guidance, inspiration, and/or strength?

_____

_____

_____

_____

_____

D. Name 3 things that are you willing to sacrifice or do in exchange for help? Rank them from most difficult to least.

_____

_____

_____

_____

E. What beliefs and skills are you already bringing to the universe in this area?

_____

_____

_____

_____

F. Once a scale of 1 - 10, how likely do you believe you'd succeed in this area without intervention? What's the basis for your estimate?

_____

_____

_____

_____

G. What serious roadblock do you need to confront in order to move forward? What's kept you from addressing this sooner?

_____

_____

_____

_____

H. About how long do you think it would take the universe to rearrange things to your favor? For instance, things like significant weight loss or a legal case could take many months to resolve.

I. _____

responded to your request.

J. In what way could your desire not align with the Universe's? For example, does someone else have an equally pressing reason for a different outcome? Is your claim superior? Why or why not?

K. How long are you willing to wait for an answer?

L. How will you cope if your spell is ineffective?

M. How you promise to thank the universe and benefit others if your spell succeeds?

PRE-SPELL PERFORMANCE

N. Describe your mood.

_____

_____

O. How relaxed are you on a scale from 1 (least relaxed) - 10? _____

P. Do you sense any potential blockages or have any concerns about your ability to successfully cast this spell??

_____

_____

_____

Q. Where will you cast this spell?

_____

R. Will anyone else be in the vicinity?

_____

S. How will you set the mood?

_____

_____

T. Are there any changes/substitutions will you be making? If so, what?

_____

_____

POST-SPELL REVIEW

U. Where you able to maintain focus and perform the spell flawlessly? If not, what happened?

_____

_____

_____

_____

V. What emotions did you feel during your preparation and performance?

_____

_____

_____

_____

W. Dreams/Other Potential Signs from the Universe | Write or Sketch below.

_____

_____

_____

_____

_____

_____

_____

_____

RESULTS

X. How would you rate your experience on a scale from 1 (negative experience) - 10 (positive experience)? _____

Y. Was the spell successful? Why or why not?

_____

_____

_____

_____

Z. If you had to cast the spell again, are there any elements (e.g. ingredients, invocation, etc.) that you'd like to adapt/change?

_____

_____

_____

SPELL: _____   **DATE:** _____

INGREDIENTS AND PREPARATION

Ideal Setting
_____

Ingredients
_____

Preparation/Instructions
_____

JOURNALING PROMPTS

A. What is your target? Why have you chosen this?

_____

_____

_____

_____

B. What sacrifice are you prepared to make?

_____

_____

_____

_____

C. Why do you feel that you need guidance, inspiration, and/or strength?

_____

_____

_____

_____

D. Name 3 things that are you willing to sacrifice or do in exchange for help? Rank them from most difficult to least.

_____

_____

_____

_____

E. What beliefs and skills are you already bringing to the universe in this area?

F. Once a scale of 1 - 10, how likely do you believe you'd succeed in this area without intervention? What's the basis for your estimate?

G. What serious roadblock do you need to confront in order to move forward? What's kept you from addressing this sooner?

H. About how long do you think it would take the universe to rearrange things to your favor? For instance, things like significant weight loss or a legal case could take many months to resolve.

I.

responded to your request.

J. In what way could your desire not align with the Universe's? For example, does someone else have an equally pressing reason for a different outcome? Is your claim superior? Why or why not?

K. How long are you willing to wait for an answer?

L. How will you cope if your spell is ineffective?

M. How you promise to thank the universe and benefit others if your spell succeeds?

PRE-SPELL PERFORMANCE

N. Describe your mood.

_____

_____

O. How relaxed are you on a scale from 1 (least relaxed) - 10? _____

P. Do you sense any potential blockages or have any concerns about your ability to successfully cast this spell??

_____

_____

_____

Q. Where will you cast this spell?

_____

R. Will anyone else be in the vicinity?

_____

S. How will you set the mood?

_____

_____

T. Are there any changes/substitutions will you be making? If so, what?

_____

_____

_____

POST-SPELL REVIEW

U. Where you able to maintain focus and perform the spell flawlessly? If not, what happened?

_____

_____

_____

_____

V. What emotions did you feel during your preparation and performance?

_____

_____

_____

_____

W. Dreams/Other Potential Signs from the Universe | Write or Sketch below.

_____

_____

_____

_____

_____

_____

_____

_____

RESULTS

X. How would you rate your experience on a scale from 1 (negative experience) - 10 (positive experience)? _____

Y. Was the spell successful? Why or why not?

_____

_____

_____

_____

Z. If you had to cast the spell again, are there any elements (e.g. ingredients, invocation, etc.) that you'd like to adapt/change?

_____

_____

_____

_____

SPELL: _____   **DATE:** _____

INGREDIENTS AND PREPARATION

Ideal Setting
_____

Ingredients
_____

Preparation/Instructions
_____

JOURNALING PROMPTS

A. What is your target? Why have you chosen this?

B. What sacrifice are you prepared to make?

C. Why do you feel that you need guidance, inspiration, and/or strength?

D. Name 3 things that are you willing to sacrifice or do in exchange for help? Rank them from most difficult to least.

E. What beliefs and skills are you already bringing to the universe in this area?

_____

_____

_____

_____

F. Once a scale of 1 - 10, how likely do you believe you'd succeed in this area without intervention? What's the basis for your estimate?

_____

_____

_____

_____

G. What serious roadblock do you need to confront in order to move forward? What's kept you from addressing this sooner?

_____

_____

_____

_____

H. About how long do you think it would take the universe to rearrange things to your favor? For instance, things like significant weight loss or a legal case could take many months to resolve.

I. _____

responded to your request.

J. In what way could your desire not align with the Universe's? For example, does someone else have an equally pressing reason for a different outcome? Is your claim superior? Why or why not?

K. How long are you willing to wait for an answer?

L. How will you cope if your spell is ineffective?

M. How you promise to thank the universe and benefit others if your spell succeeds?

PRE-SPELL PERFORMANCE

N. Describe your mood.

_____

_____

O. How relaxed are you on a scale from 1 (least relaxed) - 10? _____

P. Do you sense any potential blockages or have any concerns about your ability to successfully cast this spell??

_____

_____

_____

Q. Where will you cast this spell?

_____

R. Will anyone else be in the vicinity?

_____

S. How will you set the mood?

_____

_____

T. Are there any changes/substitutions will you be making? If so, what?

_____

_____

_____

POST-SPELL REVIEW

U. Where you able to maintain focus and perform the spell flawlessly? If not, what happened?

_____

_____

_____

_____

V. What emotions did you feel during your preparation and performance?

_____

_____

_____

_____

W. Dreams/Other Potential Signs from the Universe | Write or Sketch below.

_____

_____

_____

_____

_____

_____

_____

_____

RESULTS

X. How would you rate your experience on a scale from 1 (negative experience) - 10 (positive experience)? _____

Y. Was the spell successful? Why or why not?

_____

_____

_____

_____

Z. If you had to cast the spell again, are there any elements (e.g. ingredients, invocation, etc.) that you'd like to adapt/change?

_____

_____

_____

_____

SPELL: _____ **DATE:** _____

INGREDIENTS AND PREPARATION

Ideal Setting
_____

Ingredients
_____

Preparation/Instructions
_____

JOURNALING PROMPTS

A. What is your target? Why have you chosen this?

B. What sacrifice are you prepared to make?

C. Why do you feel that you need guidance, inspiration, and/or strength?

D. Name 3 things that are you willing to sacrifice or do in exchange for help? Rank them from most difficult to least.

E. What beliefs and skills are you already bringing to the universe in this area?

F. Once a scale of 1 - 10, how likely do you believe you'd succeed in this area without intervention? What's the basis for your estimate?

G. What serious roadblock do you need to confront in order to move forward? What's kept you from addressing this sooner?

H. About how long do you think it would take the universe to rearrange things to your favor? For instance, things like significant weight loss or a legal case could take many months to resolve.

I.

responded to your request.

J. In what way could your desire not align with the Universe's? For example, does someone else have an equally pressing reason for a different outcome? Is your claim superior? Why or why not?

K. How long are you willing to wait for an answer?

L. How will you cope if your spell is ineffective?

M. How you promise to thank the universe and benefit others if your spell succeeds?

PRE-SPELL PERFORMANCE

N. Describe your mood.

_____

_____

O. How relaxed are you on a scale from 1 (least relaxed) - 10? _____

P. Do you sense any potential blockages or have any concerns about your ability to successfully cast this spell??

_____

_____

Q. Where will you cast this spell?

_____

R. Will anyone else be in the vicinity?

_____

S. How will you set the mood?

_____

_____

T. Are there any changes/substitutions will you be making? If so, what?

_____

_____

POST-SPELL REVIEW

U. Where you able to maintain focus and perform the spell flawlessly? If not, what happened?

_____

_____

_____

_____

V. What emotions did you feel during your preparation and performance?

_____

_____

_____

_____

———————————————————————

W. Dreams/Other Potential Signs from the Universe | Write or Sketch below.

_____

_____

_____

_____

_____

_____

_____

_____

RESULTS

X. How would you rate your experience on a scale from 1 (negative experience) - 10 (positive experience)? _____

Y. Was the spell successful? Why or why not?

_____

_____

_____

_____

Z. If you had to cast the spell again, are there any elements (e.g. ingredients, invocation, etc.) that you'd like to adapt/change?

_____

_____

_____

_____

SPELL: _____ **DATE:** _____

INGREDIENTS AND PREPARATION

Ideal Setting
_____

Ingredients
_____

Preparation/Instructions
_____

JOURNALING PROMPTS

A. What is your target? Why have you chosen this?

B. What sacrifice are you prepared to make?

C. Why do you feel that you need guidance, inspiration, and/or strength?

D. Name 3 things that are you willing to sacrifice or do in exchange for help? Rank them from most difficult to least.

E. What beliefs and skills are you already bringing to the universe in this area?

F. Once a scale of 1 - 10, how likely do you believe you'd succeed in this area without intervention? What's the basis for your estimate?

G. What serious roadblock do you need to confront in order to move forward? What's kept you from addressing this sooner?

H. About how long do you think it would take the universe to rearrange things to your favor? For instance, things like significant weight loss or a legal case could take many months to resolve.

I. ---

responded to your request.

J. In what way could your desire not align with the Universe's? For example, does someone else have an equally pressing reason for a different outcome? Is your claim superior? Why or why not?

K. How long are you willing to wait for an answer?

L. How will you cope if your spell is ineffective?

M. How you promise to thank the universe and benefit others if your spell succeeds?

PRE-SPELL PERFORMANCE

N. Describe your mood.

_____

_____

O. How relaxed are you on a scale from 1 (least relaxed) - 10? _____

P. Do you sense any potential blockages or have any concerns about your ability to successfully cast this spell??

_____

_____

_____

Q. Where will you cast this spell?

_____

R. Will anyone else be in the vicinity?

_____

S. How will you set the mood?

_____

_____

T. Are there any changes/substitutions will you be making? If so, what?

_____

_____

POST-SPELL REVIEW

U. Where you able to maintain focus and perform the spell flawlessly? If not, what happened?

_____

_____

_____

_____

V. What emotions did you feel during your preparation and performance?

_____

_____

_____

_____

W. Dreams/Other Potential Signs from the Universe | Write or Sketch below.

_____

_____

_____

_____

_____

_____

_____

_____

RESULTS

X. How would you rate your experience on a scale from 1 (negative experience) - 10 (positive experience)? _____

Y. Was the spell successful? Why or why not?

Z. If you had to cast the spell again, are there any elements (e.g. ingredients, invocation, etc.) that you'd like to adapt/change?

SPELL: _____ **DATE:** _____

INGREDIENTS AND PREPARATION

Ideal Setting
_____

Ingredients
_____

Preparation/Instructions
_____

JOURNALING PROMPTS

A. What is your target? Why have you chosen this?

B. What sacrifice are you prepared to make?

C. Why do you feel that you need guidance, inspiration, and/or strength?

D. Name 3 things that are you willing to sacrifice or do in exchange for help? Rank them from most difficult to least.

E. What beliefs and skills are you already bringing to the universe in this area?

F. Once a scale of 1 - 10, how likely do you believe you'd succeed in this area without intervention? What's the basis for your estimate?

G. What serious roadblock do you need to confront in order to move forward? What's kept you from addressing this sooner?

H. About how long do you think it would take the universe to rearrange things to your favor? For instance, things like significant weight loss or a legal case could take many months to resolve.

I. responded to your request.

J. In what way could your desire not align with the Universe's? For example, does someone else have an equally pressing reason for a different outcome? Is your claim superior? Why or why not?

K. How long are you willing to wait for an answer?

L. How will you cope if your spell is ineffective?

M. How you promise to thank the universe and benefit others if your spell succeeds?

PRE-SPELL PERFORMANCE

N. Describe your mood.

_____

_____

O. How relaxed are you on a scale from 1 (least relaxed) - 10? _____

P. Do you sense any potential blockages or have any concerns about your ability to successfully cast this spell??

_____

_____

_____

Q. Where will you cast this spell?

_____

R. Will anyone else be in the vicinity?

_____

S. How will you set the mood?

_____

_____

T. Are there any changes/substitutions will you be making? If so, what?

_____

_____

_____

POST-SPELL REVIEW

U. Where you able to maintain focus and perform the spell flawlessly? If not, what happened?

_____

_____

_____

_____

V. What emotions did you feel during your preparation and performance?

_____

_____

_____

_____

W. Dreams/Other Potential Signs from the Universe I Write or Sketch below.

_____

_____

_____

_____

_____

_____

_____

_____

_____

RESULTS

X. How would you rate your experience on a scale from 1 (negative experience) - 10 (positive experience)? _____

Y. Was the spell successful? Why or why not?

_____

_____

_____

_____

Z. If you had to cast the spell again, are there any elements (e.g. ingredients, invocation, etc.) that you'd like to adapt/change?

_____

_____

_____

_____

SPELL: _____ **DATE:** _____

INGREDIENTS AND PREPARATION

Ideal Setting
_____

Ingredients
_____

Preparation/Instructions
_____

JOURNALING PROMPTS

A. What is your target? Why have you chosen this?

B. What sacrifice are you prepared to make?

C. Why do you feel that you need guidance, inspiration, and/or strength?

D. Name 3 things that are you willing to sacrifice or do in exchange for help? Rank them from most difficult to least.

E. What beliefs and skills are you already bringing to the universe in this area?

_____

_____

_____

_____

F. Once a scale of 1 - 10, how likely do you believe you'd succeed in this area without intervention? What's the basis for your estimate?

_____

_____

_____

_____

G. What serious roadblock do you need to confront in order to move forward? What's kept you from addressing this sooner?

_____

_____

_____

_____

H. About how long do you think it would take the universe to rearrange things to your favor? For instance, things like significant weight loss or a legal case could take many months to resolve.

I. _____

responded to your request.

_____

_____

_____

_____

_____

_____

_____

_____

J. In what way could your desire not align with the Universe's? For example, does someone else have an equally pressing reason for a different outcome? Is your claim superior? Why or why not?

_____

_____

_____

_____

_____

K. How long are you willing to wait for an answer?

_____

L. How will you cope if your spell is ineffective?

_____

_____

_____

_____

M. How you promise to thank the universe and benefit others if your spell succeeds?

PRE-SPELL PERFORMANCE

N. Describe your mood.

_____

_____

O. How relaxed are you on a scale from 1 (least relaxed) - 10? _____

P. Do you sense any potential blockages or have any concerns about your ability to successfully cast this spell??

_____

_____

_____

Q. Where will you cast this spell?

_____

R. Will anyone else be in the vicinity?

_____

S. How will you set the mood?

_____

_____

T. Are there any changes/substitutions will you be making? If so, what?

_____

_____

POST-SPELL REVIEW

U. Where you able to maintain focus and perform the spell flawlessly? If not, what happened?

_____

_____

_____

_____

V. What emotions did you feel during your preparation and performance?

_____

_____

_____

_____

W. Dreams/Other Potential Signs from the Universe | Write or Sketch below.

_____

_____

_____

_____

_____

_____

_____

_____

RESULTS

X. How would you rate your experience on a scale from 1 (negative experience) - 10 (positive experience)? _____

Y. Was the spell successful? Why or why not?

_____

_____

_____

_____

Z. If you had to cast the spell again, are there any elements (e.g. ingredients, invocation, etc.) that you'd like to adapt/change?

_____

_____

_____

SPELL: _____   **DATE:** _____

INGREDIENTS AND PREPARATION

Ideal Setting
_____

Ingredients
_____

Preparation/Instructions
_____

JOURNALING PROMPTS

A. What is your target? Why have you chosen this?

_____

_____

_____

_____

B. What sacrifice are you prepared to make?

_____

_____

_____

_____

C. Why do you feel that you need guidance, inspiration, and/or strength?

_____

_____

_____

_____

D. Name 3 things that are you willing to sacrifice or do in exchange for help? Rank them from most difficult to least.

_____

_____

_____

_____

E. What beliefs and skills are you already bringing to the universe in this area?

F. Once a scale of 1 - 10, how likely do you believe you'd succeed in this area without intervention? What's the basis for your estimate?

G. What serious roadblock do you need to confront in order to move forward? What's kept you from addressing this sooner?

H. About how long do you think it would take the universe to rearrange things to your favor? For instance, things like significant weight loss or a legal case could take many months to resolve.

I. responded to your request.

J. In what way could your desire not align with the Universe's? For example, does someone else have an equally pressing reason for a different outcome? Is your claim superior? Why or why not?

K. How long are you willing to wait for an answer?

L. How will you cope if your spell is ineffective?

M. How you promise to thank the universe and benefit others if your spell succeeds?

PRE-SPELL PERFORMANCE

N. Describe your mood.

_____

_____

O. How relaxed are you on a scale from 1 (least relaxed) - 10? _____

P. Do you sense any potential blockages or have any concerns about your ability to successfully cast this spell??

_____

_____

_____

Q. Where will you cast this spell?

_____

R. Will anyone else be in the vicinity?

_____

S. How will you set the mood?

_____

_____

T. Are there any changes/substitutions will you be making? If so, what?

_____

_____

_____

POST-SPELL REVIEW

U. Where you able to maintain focus and perform the spell flawlessly? If not, what happened?

_____

_____

_____

_____

V. What emotions did you feel during your preparation and performance?

_____

_____

_____

_____

_____

W. Dreams/Other Potential Signs from the Universe I Write or Sketch below.

_____

_____

_____

_____

_____

_____

_____

_____

_____

RESULTS

X. How would you rate your experience on a scale from 1 (negative experience) - 10 (positive experience)? _____

Y. Was the spell successful? Why or why not?

_____

_____

_____

_____

Z. If you had to cast the spell again, are there any elements (e.g. ingredients, invocation, etc.) that you'd like to adapt/change?

_____

_____

_____

_____

SPELL: _____ **DATE:** _____

INGREDIENTS AND PREPARATION

Ideal Setting
_____

Ingredients
_____

Preparation/Instructions
_____

JOURNALING PROMPTS

A. What is your target? Why have you chosen this?

_____

_____

_____

_____

B. What sacrifice are you prepared to make?

_____

_____

_____

_____

C. Why do you feel that you need guidance, inspiration, and/or strength?

_____

_____

_____

_____

D. Name 3 things that are you willing to sacrifice or do in exchange for help? Rank them from most difficult to least.

_____

_____

_____

_____

E. What beliefs and skills are you already bringing to the universe in this area?

F. Once a scale of 1 - 10, how likely do you believe you'd succeed in this area without intervention? What's the basis for your estimate?

G. What serious roadblock do you need to confront in order to move forward? What's kept you from addressing this sooner?

H. About how long do you think it would take the universe to rearrange things to your favor? For instance, things like significant weight loss or a legal case could take many months to resolve.

I.

responded to your request.

J. In what way could your desire not align with the Universe's? For example, does someone else have an equally pressing reason for a different outcome? Is your claim superior? Why or why not?

K. How long are you willing to wait for an answer?

L. How will you cope if your spell is ineffective?

M. How you promise to thank the universe and benefit others if your spell succeeds?

PRE-SPELL PERFORMANCE

N. Describe your mood.

_____

_____

O. How relaxed are you on a scale from 1 (least relaxed) - 10? _____

P. Do you sense any potential blockages or have any concerns about your ability to successfully cast this spell??

_____

_____

_____

Q. Where will you cast this spell?

_____

R. Will anyone else be in the vicinity?

_____

S. How will you set the mood?

_____

_____

T. Are there any changes/substitutions will you be making? If so, what?

_____

_____

POST-SPELL REVIEW

U. Where you able to maintain focus and perform the spell flawlessly? If not, what happened?

_____

_____

_____

_____

V. What emotions did you feel during your preparation and performance?

_____

_____

_____

_____

W. Dreams/Other Potential Signs from the Universe I Write or Sketch below.

_____

_____

_____

_____

_____

_____

_____

_____

_____

RESULTS

X. How would you rate your experience on a scale from 1 (negative experience) - 10 (positive experience)? _____

Y. Was the spell successful? Why or why not?

_____

_____

_____

_____

Z. If you had to cast the spell again, are there any elements (e.g. ingredients, invocation, etc.) that you'd like to adapt/change?

_____

_____

_____

SPELL: _____ **DATE:** _____

INGREDIENTS AND PREPARATION

Ideal Setting
_____

Ingredients
_____

Preparation/Instructions
_____

JOURNALING PROMPTS

A. What is your target? Why have you chosen this?

B. What sacrifice are you prepared to make?

C. Why do you feel that you need guidance, inspiration, and/or strength?

D. Name 3 things that are you willing to sacrifice or do in exchange for help? Rank them from most difficult to least.

E. What beliefs and skills are you already bringing to the universe in this area?

F. Once a scale of 1 - 10, how likely do you believe you'd succeed in this area without intervention? What's the basis for your estimate?

G. What serious roadblock do you need to confront in order to move forward? What's kept you from addressing this sooner?

H. About how long do you think it would take the universe to rearrange things to your favor? For instance, things like significant weight loss or a legal case could take many months to resolve.

I.

responded to your request.

J. In what way could your desire not align with the Universe's? For example, does someone else have an equally pressing reason for a different outcome? Is your claim superior? Why or why not?

K. How long are you willing to wait for an answer?

L. How will you cope if your spell is ineffective?

M. How you promise to thank the universe and benefit others if your spell succeeds?

PRE-SPELL PERFORMANCE

N. Describe your mood.

_____

_____

O. How relaxed are you on a scale from 1 (least relaxed) - 10? _____

P. Do you sense any potential blockages or have any concerns about your ability to successfully cast this spell??

_____

_____

_____

Q. Where will you cast this spell?

_____

R. Will anyone else be in the vicinity?

_____

S. How will you set the mood?

_____

_____

T. Are there any changes/substitutions will you be making? If so, what?

_____

_____

_____

POST-SPELL REVIEW

U. Where you able to maintain focus and perform the spell flawlessly? If not, what happened?

_____

_____

_____

V. What emotions did you feel during your preparation and performance?

_____

_____

_____

W. Dreams/Other Potential Signs from the Universe | Write or Sketch below.

_____

_____

_____

_____

_____

_____

_____

_____

RESULTS

X. How would you rate your experience on a scale from 1 (negative experience) - 10 (positive experience)? _____

Y. Was the spell successful? Why or why not?

_____

_____

_____

_____

Z. If you had to cast the spell again, are there any elements (e.g. ingredients, invocation, etc.) that you'd like to adapt/change?

_____

_____

_____

_____

SPELL: _____ **DATE:** _____

INGREDIENTS AND PREPARATION

Ideal Setting
_____

Ingredients
_____

Preparation/Instructions
_____

JOURNALING PROMPTS

A. What is your target? Why have you chosen this?

B. What sacrifice are you prepared to make?

C. Why do you feel that you need guidance, inspiration, and/or strength?

D. Name 3 things that are you willing to sacrifice or do in exchange for help? Rank them from most difficult to least.

E. What beliefs and skills are you already bringing to the universe in this area?

F. Once a scale of 1 - 10, how likely do you believe you'd succeed in this area without intervention? What's the basis for your estimate?

G. What serious roadblock do you need to confront in order to move forward? What's kept you from addressing this sooner?

H. About how long do you think it would take the universe to rearrange things to your favor? For instance, things like significant weight loss or a legal case could take many months to resolve.

I.

responded to your request.

J. In what way could your desire not align with the Universe's? For example, does someone else have an equally pressing reason for a different outcome? Is your claim superior? Why or why not?

K. How long are you willing to wait for an answer?

L. How will you cope if your spell is ineffective?

M. How you promise to thank the universe and benefit others if your spell succeeds?

PRE-SPELL PERFORMANCE

N. Describe your mood.

_____

_____

O. How relaxed are you on a scale from 1 (least relaxed) - 10? _____

P. Do you sense any potential blockages or have any concerns about your ability to successfully cast this spell??

_____

_____

_____

Q. Where will you cast this spell?

_____

R. Will anyone else be in the vicinity?

_____

S. How will you set the mood?

_____

_____

T. Are there any changes/substitutions will you be making? If so, what?

_____

_____

_____

POST-SPELL REVIEW

U. Where you able to maintain focus and perform the spell flawlessly? If not, what happened?

_____

_____

_____

_____

V. What emotions did you feel during your preparation and performance?

_____

_____

_____

_____

W. Dreams/Other Potential Signs from the Universe | Write or Sketch below.

_____

_____

_____

_____

_____

_____

_____

_____

_____

RESULTS

X. How would you rate your experience on a scale from 1 (negative experience) - 10 (positive experience)? _____

Y. Was the spell successful? Why or why not?

Z. If you had to cast the spell again, are there any elements (e.g. ingredients, invocation, etc.) that you'd like to adapt/change?

SPELL: _____   **DATE:** _____

INGREDIENTS AND PREPARATION

Ideal Setting
_____

Ingredients
_____

Preparation/Instructions
_____

JOURNALING PROMPTS

A. What is your target? Why have you chosen this?

_____

_____

_____

_____

_____

B. What sacrifice are you prepared to make?

_____

_____

_____

_____

_____

C. Why do you feel that you need guidance, inspiration, and/or strength?

_____

_____

_____

_____

_____

D. Name 3 things that are you willing to sacrifice or do in exchange for help? Rank them from most difficult to least.

_____

_____

_____

_____

E. What beliefs and skills are you already bringing to the universe in this area?

_____

_____

_____

_____

F. Once a scale of 1 - 10, how likely do you believe you'd succeed in this area without intervention? What's the basis for your estimate?

_____

_____

_____

_____

G. What serious roadblock do you need to confront in order to move forward? What's kept you from addressing this sooner?

_____

_____

_____

_____

H. About how long do you think it would take the universe to rearrange things to your favor? For instance, things like significant weight loss or a legal case could take many months to resolve.

I. _____

responded to your request.

J. In what way could your desire not align with the Universe's? For example, does someone else have an equally pressing reason for a different outcome? Is your claim superior? Why or why not?

K. How long are you willing to wait for an answer?

L. How will you cope if your spell is ineffective?

M. How you promise to thank the universe and benefit others if your spell succeeds?

PRE-SPELL PERFORMANCE

N. Describe your mood.

_____

_____

O. How relaxed are you on a scale from 1 (least relaxed) - 10? _____

P. Do you sense any potential blockages or have any concerns about your ability to successfully cast this spell??

_____

_____

_____

Q. Where will you cast this spell?

_____

R. Will anyone else be in the vicinity?

_____

S. How will you set the mood?

_____

_____

T. Are there any changes/substitutions will you be making? If so, what?

_____

_____

POST-SPELL REVIEW

U. Where you able to maintain focus and perform the spell flawlessly? If not, what happened?

_____

_____

_____

_____

V. What emotions did you feel during your preparation and performance?

_____

_____

_____

_____

W. Dreams/Other Potential Signs from the Universe | Write or Sketch below.

_____

_____

_____

_____

_____

_____

_____

_____

_____

RESULTS

X. How would you rate your experience on a scale from 1 (negative experience) - 10 (positive experience)? _____

Y. Was the spell successful? Why or why not?

_____

_____

_____

_____

Z. If you had to cast the spell again, are there any elements (e.g. ingredients, invocation, etc.) that you'd like to adapt/change?

_____

_____

_____

_____

SPELL: _____ **DATE:** _____

INGREDIENTS AND PREPARATION

Ideal Setting
_____

Ingredients
_____

Preparation/Instructions
_____

JOURNALING PROMPTS

A. What is your target? Why have you chosen this?

_____
_____
_____
_____
_____

B. What sacrifice are you prepared to make?

_____
_____
_____
_____
_____

C. Why do you feel that you need guidance, inspiration, and/or strength?

_____
_____
_____
_____

D. Name 3 things that are you willing to sacrifice or do in exchange for help? Rank them from most difficult to least.

_____
_____
_____
_____

E. What beliefs and skills are you already bringing to the universe in this area?

F. Once a scale of 1 - 10, how likely do you believe you'd succeed in this area without intervention? What's the basis for your estimate?

G. What serious roadblock do you need to confront in order to move forward? What's kept you from addressing this sooner?

H. About how long do you think it would take the universe to rearrange things to your favor? For instance, things like significant weight loss or a legal case could take many months to resolve.

I.

responded to your request.

J. In what way could your desire not align with the Universe's? For example, does someone else have an equally pressing reason for a different outcome? Is your claim superior? Why or why not?

K. How long are you willing to wait for an answer?

L. How will you cope if your spell is ineffective?

M. How you promise to thank the universe and benefit others if your spell succeeds?

PRE-SPELL PERFORMANCE

N. Describe your mood.

_____

_____

O. How relaxed are you on a scale from 1 (least relaxed) - 10? _____

P. Do you sense any potential blockages or have any concerns about your ability to successfully cast this spell??

_____

_____

_____

Q. Where will you cast this spell?

_____

R. Will anyone else be in the vicinity?

_____

S. How will you set the mood?

_____

_____

T. Are there any changes/substitutions will you be making? If so, what?

_____

_____

POST-SPELL REVIEW

U. Where you able to maintain focus and perform the spell flawlessly? If not, what happened?

_____

_____

_____

_____

V. What emotions did you feel during your preparation and performance?

_____

_____

_____

_____

W. Dreams/Other Potential Signs from the Universe | Write or Sketch below.

_____

_____

_____

_____

_____

_____

_____

_____

RESULTS

X. How would you rate your experience on a scale from 1 (negative experience) - 10 (positive experience)? _____

Y. Was the spell successful? Why or why not?

_____

_____

_____

_____

Z. If you had to cast the spell again, are there any elements (e.g. ingredients, invocation, etc.) that you'd like to adapt/change?

_____

_____

_____

_____

SPELL: _____ **DATE:** _____

INGREDIENTS AND PREPARATION

Ideal Setting

_____

Ingredients

_____

Preparation/Instructions

_____

JOURNALING PROMPTS

A. What is your target? Why have you chosen this?

_____

_____

_____

_____

_____

B. What sacrifice are you prepared to make?

_____

_____

_____

_____

_____

C. Why do you feel that you need guidance, inspiration, and/or strength?

_____

_____

_____

_____

_____

D. Name 3 things that are you willing to sacrifice or do in exchange for help? Rank them from most difficult to least.

_____

_____

_____

_____

_____

E. What beliefs and skills are you already bringing to the universe in this area?

F. Once a scale of 1 - 10, how likely do you believe you'd succeed in this area without intervention? What's the basis for your estimate?

G. What serious roadblock do you need to confront in order to move forward? What's kept you from addressing this sooner?

H. About how long do you think it would take the universe to rearrange things to your favor? For instance, things like significant weight loss or a legal case could take many months to resolve.

I.

responded to your request.

J. In what way could your desire not align with the Universe's? For example, does someone else have an equally pressing reason for a different outcome? Is your claim superior? Why or why not?

K. How long are you willing to wait for an answer?

L. How will you cope if your spell is ineffective?

M. How you promise to thank the universe and benefit others if your spell succeeds?

PRE-SPELL PERFORMANCE

N. Describe your mood.

_____

_____

O. How relaxed are you on a scale from 1 (least relaxed) - 10? _____

P. Do you sense any potential blockages or have any concerns about your ability to successfully cast this spell??

_____

_____

_____

Q. Where will you cast this spell?

_____

R. Will anyone else be in the vicinity?

_____

S. How will you set the mood?

_____

_____

T. Are there any changes/substitutions will you be making? If so, what?

_____

_____

POST-SPELL REVIEW

U. Where you able to maintain focus and perform the spell flawlessly? If not, what happened?

_____

_____

_____

_____

V. What emotions did you feel during your preparation and performance?

_____

_____

_____

_____

W. Dreams/Other Potential Signs from the Universe | Write or Sketch below.

_____

_____

_____

_____

_____

_____

_____

_____

_____

RESULTS

X. How would you rate your experience on a scale from 1 (negative experience) - 10 (positive experience)? _____

Y. Was the spell successful? Why or why not?

_____

_____

_____

_____

Z. If you had to cast the spell again, are there any elements (e.g. ingredients, invocation, etc.) that you'd like to adapt/change?

_____

_____

_____

SPELL: _____ **DATE:** _____

INGREDIENTS AND PREPARATION

Ideal Setting
_____

Ingredients
_____

Preparation/Instructions
_____

JOURNALING PROMPTS

A. What is your target? Why have you chosen this?

B. What sacrifice are you prepared to make?

C. Why do you feel that you need guidance, inspiration, and/or strength?

D. Name 3 things that are you willing to sacrifice or do in exchange for help? Rank them from most difficult to least.

E. What beliefs and skills are you already bringing to the universe in this area?

F. Once a scale of 1 - 10, how likely do you believe you'd succeed in this area without intervention? What's the basis for your estimate?

G. What serious roadblock do you need to confront in order to move forward? What's kept you from addressing this sooner?

H. About how long do you think it would take the universe to rearrange things to your favor? For instance, things like significant weight loss or a legal case could take many months to resolve.

I.

responded to your request.

J. In what way could your desire not align with the Universe's? For example, does someone else have an equally pressing reason for a different outcome? Is your claim superior? Why or why not?

K. How long are you willing to wait for an answer?

L. How will you cope if your spell is ineffective?

M. How you promise to thank the universe and benefit others if your spell succeeds?

PRE-SPELL PERFORMANCE

N. Describe your mood.

_____

_____

O. How relaxed are you on a scale from 1 (least relaxed) - 10? _____

P. Do you sense any potential blockages or have any concerns about your ability to successfully cast this spell??

_____

_____

_____

Q. Where will you cast this spell?

_____

R. Will anyone else be in the vicinity?

_____

S. How will you set the mood?

_____

_____

T. Are there any changes/substitutions will you be making? If so, what?

_____

_____

_____

POST-SPELL REVIEW

U. Where you able to maintain focus and perform the spell flawlessly? If not, what happened?

_____

_____

_____

_____

V. What emotions did you feel during your preparation and performance?

_____

_____

_____

_____

W. Dreams/Other Potential Signs from the Universe | Write or Sketch below.

_____

_____

_____

_____

_____

_____

_____

_____

_____

RESULTS

X. How would you rate your experience on a scale from 1 (negative experience) - 10 (positive experience)? _____

Y. Was the spell successful? Why or why not?

_____

_____

_____

_____

Z. If you had to cast the spell again, are there any elements (e.g. ingredients, invocation, etc.) that you'd like to adapt/change?

_____

_____

_____

_____

SPELL: _____ **DATE:** _____

INGREDIENTS AND PREPARATION

Ideal Setting

_____

Ingredients

_____

Preparation/Instructions

_____

JOURNALING PROMPTS

A. What is your target? Why have you chosen this?

B. What sacrifice are you prepared to make?

C. Why do you feel that you need guidance, inspiration, and/or strength?

D. Name 3 things that are you willing to sacrifice or do in exchange for help? Rank them from most difficult to least.

E. What beliefs and skills are you already bringing to the universe in this area?

F. Once a scale of 1 - 10, how likely do you believe you'd succeed in this area without intervention? What's the basis for your estimate?

G. What serious roadblock do you need to confront in order to move forward? What's kept you from addressing this sooner?

H. About how long do you think it would take the universe to rearrange things to your favor? For instance, things like significant weight loss or a legal case could take many months to resolve.

I.

responded to your request.

J. In what way could your desire not align with the Universe's? For example, does someone else have an equally pressing reason for a different outcome? Is your claim superior? Why or why not?

K. How long are you willing to wait for an answer?

L. How will you cope if your spell is ineffective?

M. How you promise to thank the universe and benefit others if your spell succeeds?

PRE-SPELL PERFORMANCE

N. Describe your mood.

_____

_____

O. How relaxed are you on a scale from 1 (least relaxed) - 10? _____

P. Do you sense any potential blockages or have any concerns about your ability to successfully cast this spell??

_____

_____

_____

Q. Where will you cast this spell?

_____

R. Will anyone else be in the vicinity?

_____

S. How will you set the mood?

_____

_____

T. Are there any changes/substitutions will you be making? If so, what?

_____

_____

POST-SPELL REVIEW

U. Where you able to maintain focus and perform the spell flawlessly? If not, what happened?

_____

_____

_____

_____

V. What emotions did you feel during your preparation and performance?

_____

_____

_____

_____

W. Dreams/Other Potential Signs from the Universe I Write or Sketch below.

_____

_____

_____

_____

_____

_____

_____

_____

_____

RESULTS

X. How would you rate your experience on a scale from 1 (negative experience) - 10 (positive experience)? _____

Y. Was the spell successful? Why or why not?

_____

_____

_____

_____

Z. If you had to cast the spell again, are there any elements (e.g. ingredients, invocation, etc.) that you'd like to adapt/change?

_____

_____

_____

_____

SPELL: _____   **DATE:** _____

INGREDIENTS AND PREPARATION

Ideal Setting
_____

Ingredients
_____

Preparation/Instructions
_____

JOURNALING PROMPTS

A. What is your target? Why have you chosen this?

_____

_____

_____

_____

B. What sacrifice are you prepared to make?

_____

_____

_____

_____

C. Why do you feel that you need guidance, inspiration, and/or strength?

_____

_____

_____

_____

D. Name 3 things that are you willing to sacrifice or do in exchange for help? Rank them from most difficult to least.

_____

_____

_____

_____

E. What beliefs and skills are you already bringing to the universe in this area?

F. Once a scale of 1 - 10, how likely do you believe you'd succeed in this area without intervention? What's the basis for your estimate?

G. What serious roadblock do you need to confront in order to move forward? What's kept you from addressing this sooner?

H. About how long do you think it would take the universe to rearrange things to your favor? For instance, things like significant weight loss or a legal case could take many months to resolve.

I.

responded to your request.

J. In what way could your desire not align with the Universe's? For example, does someone else have an equally pressing reason for a different outcome? Is your claim superior? Why or why not?

K. How long are you willing to wait for an answer?

L. How will you cope if your spell is ineffective?

M. How you promise to thank the universe and benefit others if your spell succeeds?

PRE-SPELL PERFORMANCE

N. Describe your mood.

_____

_____

O. How relaxed are you on a scale from 1 (least relaxed) - 10? _____

P. Do you sense any potential blockages or have any concerns about your ability to successfully cast this spell??

_____

_____

_____

Q. Where will you cast this spell?

_____

R. Will anyone else be in the vicinity?

_____

S. How will you set the mood?

_____

_____

T. Are there any changes/substitutions will you be making? If so, what?

_____

_____

_____

POST-SPELL REVIEW

U. Where you able to maintain focus and perform the spell flawlessly? If not, what happened?

_____

_____

_____

_____

V. What emotions did you feel during your preparation and performance?

_____

_____

_____

_____

W. Dreams/Other Potential Signs from the Universe | Write or Sketch below.

_____

_____

_____

_____

_____

_____

_____

_____

RESULTS

X. How would you rate your experience on a scale from 1 (negative experience) - 10 (positive experience)? _____

Y. Was the spell successful? Why or why not?

_____

_____

_____

_____

Z. If you had to cast the spell again, are there any elements (e.g. ingredients, invocation, etc.) that you'd like to adapt/change?

_____

_____

_____

SPELL: _____   **DATE:** _____

INGREDIENTS AND PREPARATION

Ideal Setting
_____

Ingredients
_____

Preparation/Instructions
_____

JOURNALING PROMPTS

A. What is your target? Why have you chosen this?

_____

_____

_____

_____

B. What sacrifice are you prepared to make?

_____

_____

_____

_____

C. Why do you feel that you need guidance, inspiration, and/or strength?

_____

_____

_____

_____

D. Name 3 things that are you willing to sacrifice or do in exchange for help? Rank them from most difficult to least.

_____

_____

_____

_____

E. What beliefs and skills are you already bringing to the universe in this area?

F. Once a scale of 1 - 10, how likely do you believe you'd succeed in this area without intervention? What's the basis for your estimate?

G. What serious roadblock do you need to confront in order to move forward? What's kept you from addressing this sooner?

H. About how long do you think it would take the universe to rearrange things to your favor? For instance, things like significant weight loss or a legal case could take many months to resolve.

I.

responded to your request.

_____

J. In what way could your desire not align with the Universe's? For example, does someone else have an equally pressing reason for a different outcome? Is your claim superior? Why or why not?

_____

K. How long are you willing to wait for an answer?

_____

L. How will you cope if your spell is ineffective?

_____

M. How you promise to thank the universe and benefit others if your spell succeeds?

PRE-SPELL PERFORMANCE

N. Describe your mood.

_____

_____

O. How relaxed are you on a scale from 1 (least relaxed) - 10? _____

P. Do you sense any potential blockages or have any concerns about your ability to successfully cast this spell??

_____

_____

_____

Q. Where will you cast this spell?

_____

R. Will anyone else be in the vicinity?

_____

S. How will you set the mood?

_____

_____

T. Are there any changes/substitutions will you be making? If so, what?

_____

_____

_____

POST-SPELL REVIEW

U. Where you able to maintain focus and perform the spell flawlessly? If not, what happened?

V. What emotions did you feel during your preparation and performance?

W. Dreams/Other Potential Signs from the Universe I Write or Sketch below.

RESULTS

X. How would you rate your experience on a scale from 1 (negative experience) - 10 (positive experience)? _____

Y. Was the spell successful? Why or why not?

Z. If you had to cast the spell again, are there any elements (e.g. ingredients, invocation, etc.) that you'd like to adapt/change?

SPELL: _____ **DATE:** _____

INGREDIENTS AND PREPARATION

Ideal Setting
_____

Ingredients
_____

Preparation/Instructions
_____

JOURNALING PROMPTS

A. What is your target? Why have you chosen this?

_____

_____

_____

_____

B. What sacrifice are you prepared to make?

_____

_____

_____

_____

C. Why do you feel that you need guidance, inspiration, and/or strength?

_____

_____

_____

_____

D. Name 3 things that are you willing to sacrifice or do in exchange for help? Rank them from most difficult to least.

_____

_____

_____

_____

E. What beliefs and skills are you already bringing to the universe in this area?

F. Once a scale of 1 - 10, how likely do you believe you'd succeed in this area without intervention? What's the basis for your estimate?

G. What serious roadblock do you need to confront in order to move forward? What's kept you from addressing this sooner?

H. About how long do you think it would take the universe to rearrange things to your favor? For instance, things like significant weight loss or a legal case could take many months to resolve.

I.

responded to your request.

J. In what way could your desire not align with the Universe's? For example, does someone else have an equally pressing reason for a different outcome? Is your claim superior? Why or why not?

K. How long are you willing to wait for an answer?

L. How will you cope if your spell is ineffective?

M. How you promise to thank the universe and benefit others if your spell succeeds?

PRE-SPELL PERFORMANCE

N. Describe your mood.

_____

_____

O. How relaxed are you on a scale from 1 (least relaxed) - 10? _____

P. Do you sense any potential blockages or have any concerns about your ability to successfully cast this spell??

_____

_____

_____

Q. Where will you cast this spell?

_____

R. Will anyone else be in the vicinity?

_____

S. How will you set the mood?

_____

_____

T. Are there any changes/substitutions will you be making? If so, what?

_____

_____

POST-SPELL REVIEW

U. Where you able to maintain focus and perform the spell flawlessly? If not, what
    happened?

_____

_____

_____

_____

V. What emotions did you feel during your preparation and performance?

_____

_____

_____

_____

W. Dreams/Other Potential Signs from the Universe I Write or Sketch below.

_____

_____

_____

_____

_____

_____

_____

_____

_____

RESULTS

X. How would you rate your experience on a scale from 1 (negative experience) - 10 (positive experience)? _____

Y. Was the spell successful? Why or why not?

_____

_____

_____

_____

Z. If you had to cast the spell again, are there any elements (e.g. ingredients, invocation, etc.) that you'd like to adapt/change?

_____

_____

_____

SPELL: _____ **DATE:** _____

INGREDIENTS AND PREPARATION

Ideal Setting
_____

Ingredients
_____

Preparation/Instructions
_____

JOURNALING PROMPTS

A. What is your target? Why have you chosen this?

B. What sacrifice are you prepared to make?

C. Why do you feel that you need guidance, inspiration, and/or strength?

D. Name 3 things that are you willing to sacrifice or do in exchange for help? Rank them from most difficult to least.

E. What beliefs and skills are you already bringing to the universe in this area?

F. Once a scale of 1 - 10, how likely do you believe you'd succeed in this area without intervention? What's the basis for your estimate?

G. What serious roadblock do you need to confront in order to move forward? What's kept you from addressing this sooner?

H. About how long do you think it would take the universe to rearrange things to your favor? For instance, things like significant weight loss or a legal case could take many months to resolve.

I. _____

responded to your request.

J. In what way could your desire not align with the Universe's? For example, does someone else have an equally pressing reason for a different outcome? Is your claim superior? Why or why not?

K. How long are you willing to wait for an answer?

L. How will you cope if your spell is ineffective?

M. How you promise to thank the universe and benefit others if your spell succeeds?

PRE-SPELL PERFORMANCE

N. Describe your mood.

_____

_____

O. How relaxed are you on a scale from 1 (least relaxed) - 10? _____

P. Do you sense any potential blockages or have any concerns about your ability to successfully cast this spell??

_____

_____

_____

Q. Where will you cast this spell?

_____

_____

R. Will anyone else be in the vicinity?

_____

S. How will you set the mood?

_____

_____

T. Are there any changes/substitutions will you be making? If so, what?

_____

_____

POST-SPELL REVIEW

U. Where you able to maintain focus and perform the spell flawlessly? If not, what happened?

_____

_____

_____

_____

V. What emotions did you feel during your preparation and performance?

_____

_____

_____

_____

W. Dreams/Other Potential Signs from the Universe I Write or Sketch below.

_____

_____

_____

_____

_____

_____

_____

_____

RESULTS

X. How would you rate your experience on a scale from 1 (negative experience) - 10 (positive experience)? _____

Y. Was the spell successful? Why or why not?

_____

_____

_____

_____

Z. If you had to cast the spell again, are there any elements (e.g. ingredients, invocation, etc.) that you'd like to adapt/change?

_____

_____

_____

_____

SPELL: _____ **DATE:** _____

INGREDIENTS AND PREPARATION

Ideal Setting
_____

Ingredients
_____

Preparation/Instructions
_____

JOURNALING PROMPTS

A. What is your target? Why have you chosen this?

B. What sacrifice are you prepared to make?

C. Why do you feel that you need guidance, inspiration, and/or strength?

D. Name 3 things that are you willing to sacrifice or do in exchange for help? Rank them from most difficult to least.

E. What beliefs and skills are you already bringing to the universe in this area?

F. Once a scale of 1 - 10, how likely do you believe you'd succeed in this area without intervention? What's the basis for your estimate?

G. What serious roadblock do you need to confront in order to move forward? What's kept you from addressing this sooner?

H. About how long do you think it would take the universe to rearrange things to your favor? For instance, things like significant weight loss or a legal case could take many months to resolve.

I.

responded to your request.

J. In what way could your desire not align with the Universe's? For example, does someone else have an equally pressing reason for a different outcome? Is your claim superior? Why or why not?

K. How long are you willing to wait for an answer?

L. How will you cope if your spell is ineffective?

M. How you promise to thank the universe and benefit others if your spell succeeds?

PRE-SPELL PERFORMANCE

N. Describe your mood.

_____

_____

O. How relaxed are you on a scale from 1 (least relaxed) - 10? _____

P. Do you sense any potential blockages or have any concerns about your ability to successfully cast this spell??

_____

_____

_____

Q. Where will you cast this spell?

_____

R. Will anyone else be in the vicinity?

_____

S. How will you set the mood?

_____

_____

T. Are there any changes/substitutions will you be making? If so, what?

_____

_____

_____

POST-SPELL REVIEW

U. Where you able to maintain focus and perform the spell flawlessly? If not, what happened?

V. What emotions did you feel during your preparation and performance?

W. Dreams/Other Potential Signs from the Universe I Write or Sketch below.

RESULTS

X. How would you rate your experience on a scale from 1 (negative experience) - 10 (positive experience)? _____

Y. Was the spell successful? Why or why not?

_____

_____

_____

_____

Z. If you had to cast the spell again, are there any elements (e.g. ingredients, invocation, etc.) that you'd like to adapt/change?

_____

_____

_____

_____

SPELL: _____   **DATE:** _____

INGREDIENTS AND PREPARATION

Ideal Setting
_____

Ingredients
_____

Preparation/Instructions
_____

JOURNALING PROMPTS

A. What is your target? Why have you chosen this?

B. What sacrifice are you prepared to make?

C. Why do you feel that you need guidance, inspiration, and/or strength?

D. Name 3 things that are you willing to sacrifice or do in exchange for help? Rank them from most difficult to least.

E. What beliefs and skills are you already bringing to the universe in this area?

_____

_____

_____

_____

F. Once a scale of 1 - 10, how likely do you believe you'd succeed in this area without intervention? What's the basis for your estimate?

_____

_____

_____

_____

G. What serious roadblock do you need to confront in order to move forward? What's kept you from addressing this sooner?

_____

_____

_____

_____

H. About how long do you think it would take the universe to rearrange things to your favor? For instance, things like significant weight loss or a legal case could take many months to resolve.

I. _____

responded to your request.

J. In what way could your desire not align with the Universe's? For example, does someone else have an equally pressing reason for a different outcome? Is your claim superior? Why or why not?

K. How long are you willing to wait for an answer?

L. How will you cope if your spell is ineffective?

M. How you promise to thank the universe and benefit others if your spell succeeds?

PRE-SPELL PERFORMANCE

N. Describe your mood.

_____

_____

O. How relaxed are you on a scale from 1 (least relaxed) - 10? _____

P. Do you sense any potential blockages or have any concerns about your ability to successfully cast this spell??

_____

_____

_____

Q. Where will you cast this spell?

_____

_____

R. Will anyone else be in the vicinity?

_____

S. How will you set the mood?

_____

_____

T. Are there any changes/substitutions will you be making? If so, what?

_____

_____

_____

POST-SPELL REVIEW

U. Where you able to maintain focus and perform the spell flawlessly? If not, what happened?

V. What emotions did you feel during your preparation and performance?

W. Dreams/Other Potential Signs from the Universe | Write or Sketch below.

RESULTS

X. How would you rate your experience on a scale from 1 (negative experience) - 10 (positive experience)? _____

Y. Was the spell successful? Why or why not?

_____

_____

_____

_____

Z. If you had to cast the spell again, are there any elements (e.g. ingredients, invocation, etc.) that you'd like to adapt/change?

_____

_____

_____

_____

SPELL: _____   **DATE:** _____

INGREDIENTS AND PREPARATION

Ideal Setting
_____

Ingredients
_____

Preparation/Instructions
_____

JOURNALING PROMPTS

A. What is your target? Why have you chosen this?

_____
_____
_____
_____

B. What sacrifice are you prepared to make?

_____
_____
_____
_____

C. Why do you feel that you need guidance, inspiration, and/or strength?

_____
_____
_____
_____

D. Name 3 things that are you willing to sacrifice or do in exchange for help? Rank them from most difficult to least.

_____
_____
_____
_____

E. What beliefs and skills are you already bringing to the universe in this area?

_____

_____

_____

_____

F. Once a scale of 1 - 10, how likely do you believe you'd succeed in this area without intervention? What's the basis for your estimate?

_____

_____

_____

_____

G. What serious roadblock do you need to confront in order to move forward? What's kept you from addressing this sooner?

_____

_____

_____

_____

H. About how long do you think it would take the universe to rearrange things to your favor? For instance, things like significant weight loss or a legal case could take many months to resolve.

I. _____

responded to your request.

_____
_____
_____
_____
_____
_____
_____

J. In what way could your desire not align with the Universe's? For example, does someone else have an equally pressing reason for a different outcome? Is your claim superior? Why or why not?

_____
_____
_____
_____
_____

K. How long are you willing to wait for an answer?

_____

L. How will you cope if your spell is ineffective?

_____
_____
_____
_____

M. How you promise to thank the universe and benefit others if your spell succeeds?

PRE-SPELL PERFORMANCE

N. Describe your mood.

_____

_____

O. How relaxed are you on a scale from 1 (least relaxed) - 10? _____

P. Do you sense any potential blockages or have any concerns about your ability to successfully cast this spell??

_____

_____

_____

Q. Where will you cast this spell?

_____

R. Will anyone else be in the vicinity?

_____

S. How will you set the mood?

_____

_____

T. Are there any changes/substitutions will you be making? If so, what?

_____

_____

_____

POST-SPELL REVIEW

U. Where you able to maintain focus and perform the spell flawlessly? If not, what happened?

_____

_____

_____

_____

V. What emotions did you feel during your preparation and performance?

_____

_____

_____

_____

W. Dreams/Other Potential Signs from the Universe | Write or Sketch below.

_____

_____

_____

_____

_____

_____

_____

_____

_____

RESULTS

X. How would you rate your experience on a scale from 1 (negative experience) - 10 (positive experience)? _____

Y. Was the spell successful? Why or why not?

Z. If you had to cast the spell again, are there any elements (e.g. ingredients, invocation, etc.) that you'd like to adapt/change?

SPELL: _____   **DATE:** _____

INGREDIENTS AND PREPARATION

Ideal Setting
_____

Ingredients
_____

Preparation/Instructions
_____

JOURNALING PROMPTS

A. What is your target? Why have you chosen this?

B. What sacrifice are you prepared to make?

C. Why do you feel that you need guidance, inspiration, and/or strength?

D. Name 3 things that are you willing to sacrifice or do in exchange for help? Rank them from most difficult to least.

E. What beliefs and skills are you already bringing to the universe in this area?

_____

_____

_____

_____

_____

F. Once a scale of 1 - 10, how likely do you believe you'd succeed in this area without intervention? What's the basis for your estimate?

_____

_____

_____

_____

G. What serious roadblock do you need to confront in order to move forward? What's kept you from addressing this sooner?

_____

_____

_____

_____

_____

H. About how long do you think it would take the universe to rearrange things to your favor? For instance, things like significant weight loss or a legal case could take many months to resolve.

I. _____

responded to your request.

J. In what way could your desire not align with the Universe's? For example, does someone else have an equally pressing reason for a different outcome? Is your claim superior? Why or why not?

K. How long are you willing to wait for an answer?

L. How will you cope if your spell is ineffective?

M. How you promise to thank the universe and benefit others if your spell succeeds?

PRE-SPELL PERFORMANCE

N. Describe your mood.

_____

_____

O. How relaxed are you on a scale from 1 (least relaxed) - 10? _____

P. Do you sense any potential blockages or have any concerns about your ability to successfully cast this spell??

_____

_____

_____

Q. Where will you cast this spell?

_____

R. Will anyone else be in the vicinity?

_____

S. How will you set the mood?

_____

_____

T. Are there any changes/substitutions will you be making? If so, what?

_____

_____

_____

POST-SPELL REVIEW

U. Where you able to maintain focus and perform the spell flawlessly? If not, what happened?

_____

_____

_____

_____

V. What emotions did you feel during your preparation and performance?

_____

_____

_____

_____

W. Dreams/Other Potential Signs from the Universe | Write or Sketch below.

_____

_____

_____

_____

_____

_____

_____

_____

RESULTS

X. How would you rate your experience on a scale from 1 (negative experience) - 10 (positive experience)? _____

Y. Was the spell successful? Why or why not?

_____

_____

_____

_____

Z. If you had to cast the spell again, are there any elements (e.g. ingredients, invocation, etc.) that you'd like to adapt/change?

_____

_____

_____

_____